Preschool Daily
Plan Book

by Sherrill B. Flora

Carson-Dellosa Publishing Company, Inc.

Credits:
Author: Sherrill B. Flora
Inside Illustrations: Julie Anderson
Cover Design: Annette Hollister-Papp
Layout Design: Mark Conrad

Hints for Planning...

LESSON PLAN SHEETS - PAGES 11–62

Taking the time to prepare and organize your daily materials is the secret to successful teaching! Teachers who carefully plan their curriculum have easier days, happier children, and will discover that more learning is taking place within the classroom.

The lesson plan pages provided in the *Preschool Daily Plan Book* allow for flexibility. The narrow column on the left-hand side of the page may be used to plan according to learning centers, curriculum areas, or by the time of day.

MONTHLY CALENDAR - PAGE 10

Make copies of the reproducible calendar to assist in planning ahead. Plot out your month with thematic units, special stories, or holiday and seasonal activities.

STUDENT INFORMATION - PAGES 4–7

The information contained within these pages is critical for an early childhood teacher. Make sure that each section is filled out for each one of your students. With the advances in technology, it is an extra plus to have a parent's e-mail address. During a busy day, it is often difficult to relay all the information you would like to provide a parent and vice versa. Communicating over the Internet allows both the parent and teacher to keep one another closely informed.

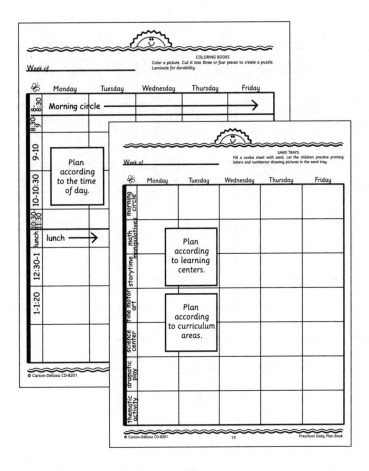

BIRTHDAY CHART - PAGE 8

Here is a handy place to record all the birthdays of the children in your class. When you are little, it is important to have your birthday remembered by the teacher.

WEB SITES - PAGE 9

A list of six early childhood Web sites is provided to assist you in your planning and professional development.

AWARDS AND INCENTIVES - PAGES 63–64

These pages contain reproducible awards and incentives designed for young children. Enjoy using them!

Student Information

Name	Days in Attendance						Parents' names	Home phone	Dad's work	Mom's work	Emergency
	M	T	W	TH	F						

Preschool Daily Plan Book

Cell phone	E-mail	Address	Other information

Student Information

Name	Days in Attendance						Parents' names	Home phone	Dad's work	Mom's work	Emergency
	M	T	W	TH	F						

Preschool Daily Plan Book

Cell phone	E-mail	Address	Other information

Preschool Daily Plan Book

Birthday Chart

January

February

March

April

May

June

July

August

September

October

November

December

Preschool Daily Plan Book

Web Sites

<u>http://www.naeyc.org</u>
National Association for the Education of Young Children

Mission statement: The National Association for the Education of Young Children (NAEYC) exists for the purpose of leading and consolidating the efforts of individuals and groups working to achieve healthy development and constructive education for all young children." Visiting this site you will be able to discover new resources, information about professional development, the position statements, accreditation, news about upcoming conferences, and so much more.

<u>http://www.eric.ed.gov</u>
ERIC (Educational Resources Information Center) Clearinghouse on Elementary and Early Childhood Education

ERIC is a national information system designed to provide users with ready access to an extensive body of education-related literature. Established in 1966, ERIC is funded by the U.S. Department of Education, Office of Educational Research and Improvement (OERI), and is administered by the National Library of Education.

<u>http://www.ecewebguide.com</u>
Early Childhood Education Web Guide

The Early Childhood Education Web Guide seeks to provide child care professionals with the most up-to-date Internet resources. The sites on this guide are checked on a weekly basis to ensure their reliability and integrity.

<u>http://www.crayola.com</u>
Crayola Crayons

The crayon manufacturer offers a wide variety of activities for children, as well as information for parents and educators. Projects include art and science.

<u>http://www.ipl.org/youth/StoryHour</u>
Internet Public Library

Internet Public Library offers some slide-show stories, some animated, some audio versions.

<u>http://www.nwf.org</u>
National Wildlife Federation

Presented by the National Wildlife Federation, this address will take you to the NWF home page. Click on Ranger Rick's Kid Zone. Scroll down and click "Your Big Backyard." This site has early learning games about animals and the earth.

Sunday	Monday	Tuesday	Wednesday	Thursday	Friday	Saturday

THE APPLE TREE
*Way up in the apple tree,
Two little apples smiled at me.
I shook that tree as hard as I could.
Down they came.
Ummmmm, they were good.*

Week of _____

	Monday	Tuesday	Wednesday	Thursday	Friday

Week of _____

	Monday	Tuesday	Wednesday	Thursday	Friday

Week of _____

	Monday	Tuesday	Wednesday	Thursday	Friday

Week of _____

	Monday	Tuesday	Wednesday	Thursday	Friday

Add a growth chart to your classroom. Mark the childrens' heights.
Discuss concepts such as, tallest, shortest, taller, shorter, same size.

Week of _____

	Monday	Tuesday	Wednesday	Thursday	Friday

COLORING BOOK PUZZLES
Color a picture. Cut it into three or four pieces to create a puzzle.
Laminate for durability.

Week of _____

	Monday	Tuesday	Wednesday	Thursday	Friday

PLAY DOUGH
1 cup salt, 2 cups flour, 6 teaspoons alum, 2 tablespoons salad oil, and 1 cup water. Mix until smooth. Add food coloring to water to give the play dough color.

<u>Week of</u> _____

	Monday	Tuesday	Wednesday	Thursday	Friday

Week of _____

	Monday	Tuesday	Wednesday	Thursday	Friday

SAND TRAYS
Fill a cookie sheet with sand. Let the children practice printing letters and numbers or drawing pictures in the sand tray.

Week of _____

	Monday	Tuesday	Wednesday	Thursday	Friday

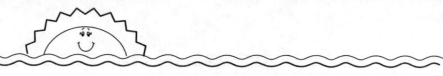

Week of _____

HICKORY DICKORY DOCK
Hickory dickory dock.
The mouse ran up the clock.
The clock struck one,
The mouse ran down.
Hickory dickory dock.

	Monday	Tuesday	Wednesday	Thursday	Friday

CARPET SQUARES
Carpet squares (samples from carpeting stores) make wonderful scooters on uncarpeted floors.

Week of _____

	Monday	Tuesday	Wednesday	Thursday	Friday

MATCHING SOUNDS
Save baby food jars. Fill two jars with the same objects (2 jars with buttons, 2 jars with rice, etc.) Child closes eyes and shakes the jars to discover which ones have the same sound.

Week of _____

	Monday	Tuesday	Wednesday	Thursday	Friday

FRUIT KABOBS
Use several types of soft or canned fruit. Cut into bite-sized pieces. Place in bowls. Provide children with plastic drinking straws. The children can skewer the fruit on the straws to create fruit kabobs.

Week of _____

	Monday	Tuesday	Wednesday	Thursday	Friday

Week of _____

MOSAICS
Colorful cereal is a great material for creating mosaic designs. Draw a circle. Fill the circle with glue and let the children create a mosaic design.

	Monday	Tuesday	Wednesday	Thursday	Friday

STORYTELLING

Have the children pantomime the actions as you read or tell a story. Example: Goldilocks "skipped" through the woods.

Week of _____

	Monday	Tuesday	Wednesday	Thursday	Friday

Week of _____

FLOUR AND SALT FINGER PAINT
1 cup flour, 1½ teaspoons salt, 1 cup water. Add food coloring to water for color. Mix. This paint has a unique texture.

	Monday	Tuesday	Wednesday	Thursday	Friday

MINI ICE CREAM SANDWICHES
Spoon vanilla ice cream onto a small shortbread butter cookie.
Place another cookie on top. Put in the freezer.

Week of _____

	Monday	Tuesday	Wednesday	Thursday	Friday

MOVEMENT RHYME

Five big elephants-oh, what a sight, swinging their trunks from left to right! Four are followers, and one is the king. But they all walk around in the big circus ring. (Pantomime.)

Week of _____

	Monday	Tuesday	Wednesday	Thursday	Friday

Week of _____

	Monday	Tuesday	Wednesday	Thursday	Friday

MAKE BUBBLES
½ cup water, ½ cup glycerin, and 1 tablespoon liquid starch. U
a bubble pipe or a straw to blow bubbles.

	Monday	Tuesday	Wednesday	Thursday	Friday

SNACK FUN
Mix together peanut butter and a small amount of chocolate syrup.
Spread on graham crackers.

<u>Week of</u> _____

	Monday	Tuesday	Wednesday	Thursday	Friday

     Preschool Daily Plan Book

Fill an egg carton with tempera paint. Place a cotton swab in each section to be used as a paintbrush. (Makes for easy clean-up!)

Week of _____

	Monday	Tuesday	Wednesday	Thursday	Friday

Week of _____

SOAP FLAKES FINGER PAINT
Beat soap flakes and water in a bowl until it is the consistency of
whipped cream. Add food coloring or tempera paint for color.

	Monday	Tuesday	Wednesday	Thursday	Friday

GRANDMOTHER'S GLASSES

These are grandmother's glasses. This is grandmother's cap. This is the way she folds her hands, and lays them in her lap. (Pantomime.)

Week of _____

	Monday	Tuesday	Wednesday	Thursday	Friday

Save boxes: shoe boxes, milk cartons, cereal boxes, etc. Cover with Con-Tact® paper. For very little expense you can have a huge building block collection.

Week of _____

	Monday	Tuesday	Wednesday	Thursday	Friday

LOUD AND SOFT SOUNDS
Play a CD. Play it loud and the children should hop. Play it soft and
the children should tip-toe.

Week of _____

	Monday	Tuesday	Wednesday	Thursday	Friday

Week of _____

	Monday	Tuesday	Wednesday	Thursday	Friday

Week of _____

OLD CATALOGS
Cut out pictures from catalogs of various categories. Glue to index cards and laminate. Use cards for sorting and classifying activities (people, furniture, clothing, food, etc.).

Monday	Tuesday	Wednesday	Thursday	Friday

WET CHALK
Draw with colored chalk on moistened construction paper.
Let dry. Spray with hair spray to keep picture from smudging.

<u>Week of</u> _____

	Monday	Tuesday	Wednesday	Thursday	Friday

Week of _____

TAPE RECORDER
Make a tape recording of the children talking. Tape recorders can encourage expressive language skills – not to mention that children love to listen to themselves.

	Monday	Tuesday	Wednesday	Thursday	Friday

FUNNY PUTTY
Mix two parts white glue with one part liquid starch. Add small amounts of starch until the texture is workable.

__Week of__ _____

	Monday	Tuesday	Wednesday	Thursday	Friday

REST TIME RHYME
We are baby robins in a nest. We are yawning. . .nodding. . .stretching. We have all been fed, and now we're in bed. We are yawning. . .nodding. . .stretching.

Week of _____

	Monday	Tuesday	Wednesday	Thursday	Friday

Make many paper footprints and laminate. The footprints can be used for creating mazes, paths, and trails that the children can follow.

Week of _____

	Monday	Tuesday	Wednesday	Thursday	Friday

Week of _____

	Monday	Tuesday	Wednesday	Thursday	Friday

Week of _____

OLD CRAYONS
Line muffin tins with foil. Fill each section with old broken crayons.
Melt in oven. Cool and you will have new "chunky" crayons.

	Monday	Tuesday	Wednesday	Thursday	Friday

MATCHING
Using scrap fabric, glue a small piece of fabric on index cards. Make sure you have two or more of each pattern. The children will enjoy matching the "same" patterns.

	Monday	Tuesday	Wednesday	Thursday	Friday

APPLIANCE BOX
Locate an appliance box. Turn the box into a classroom playhouse.

Week of _____

	Monday	Tuesday	Wednesday	Thursday	Friday

VISUAL MEMORY
Place 8 to 12 objects on a tray. Cover the tray with a cloth. Show the children the tray for about thirty seconds. Cover the tray again and ask the children to recall as many of the objects as they can.

<u>Week of</u> _____

✿	Monday	Tuesday	Wednesday	Thursday	Friday

Week of _____

NO-BAKE GRANOLA COOKIES
½ cup honey, 1 cup powdered milk, 1 cup peanut butter, granola cereal. Mix honey, powdered milk, and peanut butter together and roll into balls. Roll balls in granola cereal.

	Monday	Tuesday	Wednesday	Thursday	Friday

Week of _____

	Monday	Tuesday	Wednesday	Thursday	Friday

POURING
Children love pouring activities. Fill a water table or dish washing basin with rice. Provide all sorts of containers for pouring activities.

Week of _____

	Monday	Tuesday	Wednesday	Thursday	Friday

Week of _____

POPSICLES
Mix 2 cups vanilla yogurt and 8 ounces orange juice. Pour in an ice cube tray or small paper cups. Add sticks before the mixture is completely frozen.

	Monday	Tuesday	Wednesday	Thursday	Friday

Week of ______________________

SHAVING CREAM FINGER PAINT

Squirt shaving cream on a Formica countertop. Add a small amount of powered tempera paint. Let the children make designs on the table. Just wipe up to clean up.

	Monday	Tuesday	Wednesday	Thursday	Friday

EGG CARTONS
Save egg cartons. Use for sorting. You can also store materials in the cartons.

	Monday	Tuesday	Wednesday	Thursday	Friday

Week of _____

	Monday	Tuesday	Wednesday	Thursday	Friday

Week of _____

	Monday	Tuesday	Wednesday	Thursday	Friday

FINGER JELL-O
Combine 2 envelopes of unflavored gelatin and 2 packages of Jell-O gelatin with 2 cups of hot water. Add 2 cups of cold water. Pour in a cookie sheet and chill. Cut into shapes with cookie cutters.

Week of _____

	Monday	Tuesday	Wednesday	Thursday	Friday

Week of _____

	Monday	Tuesday	Wednesday	Thursday	Friday

Week of _____

	Monday	Tuesday	Wednesday	Thursday	Friday

PAPER PLATE MASKS
Draw and color a face on a paper plate. The teacher cuts out ey
holes. Tape plate to a paint stir stick so the plate can be held i
front of a face.

Week of _____

	Monday	Tuesday	Wednesday	Thursday	Friday

Week of _____

	Monday	Tuesday	Wednesday	Thursday	Friday

Week of _____

EENCY WEENCY SPIDER
The eency weency spider went up the water spout.
Down came the rain and washed the spider out.
Out came the sun and dried up all the rain.
And the eency weency spider went up the spout again.
(With hand actions.)

	Monday	Tuesday	Wednesday	Thursday	Friday

Preschool Daily Plan Book

This is what I did today.

_____

_____

_____

_____

_____

_____

date _____

My teacher is so proud of me!

I was dry all day!

I was a great friend today!

Reminder Note:

Don't forget

_____

_____

_____

_____

_____

_____

_____

_____

Happy Birthday to:

_____

Happy Birthday to you!

Happy Birthday Dear _____!

Happy Birthday to you!

From your teacher _____.